TORNADO!
POEMS

Also by Arnold Adoff / Ronald Himler

make a circle   keep us   in
                        poems for a good day

TORNADO!
POEMS

Arnold Adoff

Illustrated by Ronald Himler

Delacorte Press / New York

Some of the poems in this book first appeared in Cricket magazine

Text Copyright © 1976, 1977 by Arnold Adoff

Illustrations Copyright © 1977 by Ronald Himler

Manufactured in the United States of America

First printing

Library of Congress Cataloging in Publication Data

Adoff, Arnold.
    Tornado!

    SUMMARY: A poetic description of a tornado and its aftermath.
    1. Tornadoes – Juvenile poetry. [1. Tornadoes – Poetry] I. Himler, Ronald. II. Title.
PZ8.3.A233To   811'.5'4   76-47241
ISBN 0-440-08964-6
ISBN 0-440-08965-4 lib. bdg.

For Leigh and Jaime
       and their
  young
      sisters and brothers
      of
        Xenia, Ohio

For Andy, Warren, Les, Gary,
      and
      all the men and women
      who
        rushed in to
           do
the work of rescue
      and
        recovery

          A.A.

from the dictionary

a violent   whirling
                    wind
      especially
                         in the central
united
states
      accompanied by a rapidly
                              rotating
funnel
shaped
cloud
            that usually   destroys

            everything
            along its narrow
                              path

from the spanish

                    tronada
thunder
thunderstorm

                    tronar
to thunder
                    and
                    tornar
to turn

                    tornado

TORNADO!
POEMS

each spring season

beginning in march
        with its cool rains
            through the warm afternoons
of may and june

the storms head north
        along a line
                        hundreds of miles
                long and wide
called   tornado valley

warm air meeting cold air from canada
        high above the land and people
warm air from
                        texas and louisiana
            through alabama and georgia
            through tennessee and kentucky
and indiana   and into
                        ohio
where we live

lines of storm clouds full

      of lightning and thunder
rain   and sometimes hail
              high winds
     and sometimes from these storms

black and whirling clouds
    may form
     dip down
their funnel bottoms

           touch
the land
   and rise again

on the news at noon

the radar
          shows this curving cloud
in the shape of a puffy   number six

the man says they almost always come
   from the south   west
   so you should lie down
      in the south   west
                          corner
of your basement
                  and cover up
or get to a place in the center
               of the house

if it hits
   it will blow your house away
from you
            and none of the stuff
            will crash on your
                          head

after he names other towns

the man   names our town
        and points to us
we are
      here
this   dot on the radar screen

he says the curving cloud
  will be coming
           soon
to us

then the storm does come

and it gets dark
    the thunder
    the lightning
  come real close
become real

momma says
        we have to unplug the television
        we have to unclip the roof
            antenna wires
      from in back of the set
because of the lightning
        danger

then all we have is brother's
      mickey   mouse
           radio

      mickey gives us the news
old   mickey
        sees us through

in our center

of the house
            we are throwing the pots
                        and pans
out of the bottom cabinets

            the sound of hail
            in a small   room
but
    under the sink
    is warm   like
            kentucky caves

            with doors

daddy walks

around
        from room to room
looking
        out the windows
at the hail stones
            covering the ground
looking at the sky

        because the noise
                    is strong
he puts his hand against one ear
            his head down low
and mickey up against the other
                        ear
for news

momma is saying

we will be o k
we
        will be o k
over
and
over

louder and louder
        and telling
dad
        to get away from the
                windows
like
a
fool

momma says

always remember that it's good
to be afraid
            when there is something
that can hurt
            when there is
some danger
            and you want to have your head
            come out all round
                    and whole
a one piece
        head

if you hold

your self
     tight together
and   listen

      you can hear the danger

if you hold
your self
     tight together
and   listen

     my feet are hot

    afraid   can be full
         of life

    and my hands
             are
             ice

           and
           wet

   and my hands
   are
      holding
      my
        hands

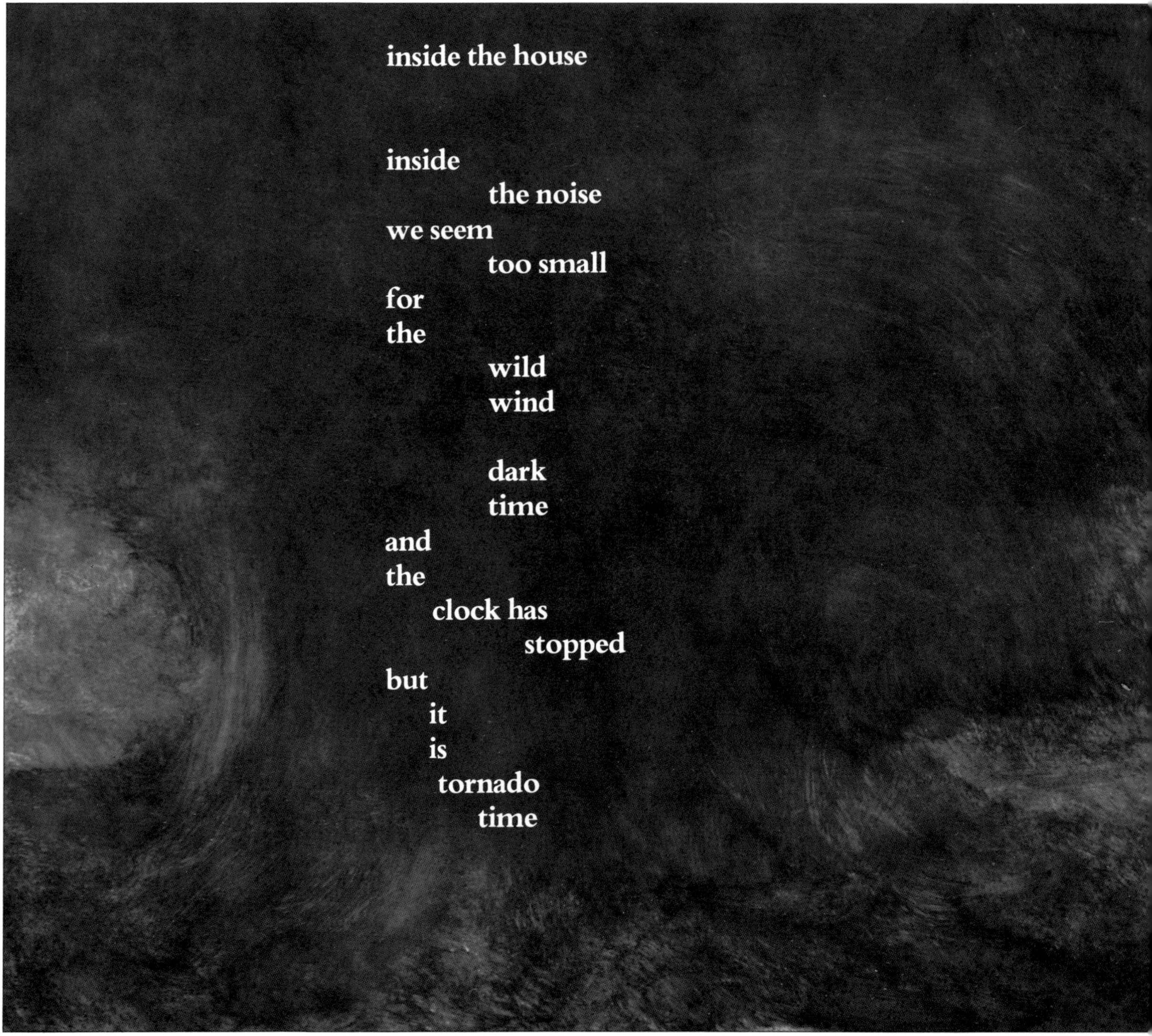

inside the house

inside
      the noise
we seem
      too small
for
the
      wild
      wind

      dark
      time
and
the
   clock has
      stopped
but
  it
  is
  tornado
    time

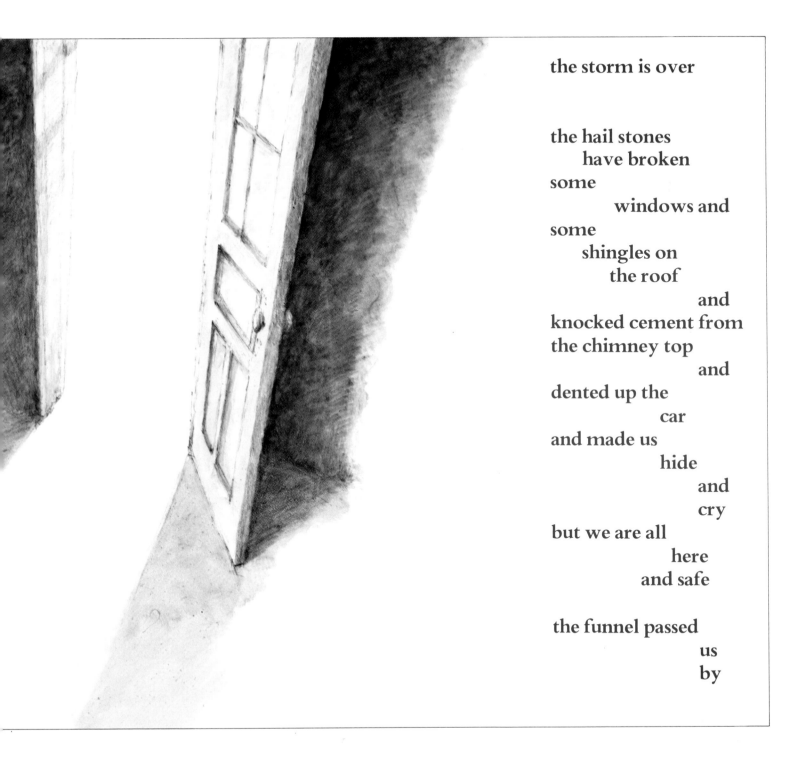

the storm is over

the hail stones
   have broken
some
      windows and
some
   shingles on
    the roof
      and
knocked cement from
the chimney top
      and
dented up the
    car
and made us
    hide
    and
    cry
but we are all
    here
  and safe

the funnel passed
    us
    by

after the storm passes

we run
            outside
to collect hail stones
big as tennis   balls
and hard as
                    rocks

big
as all the noise they made
and starting to melt in the
                              sun

we take some
for the
            freezer

the sun feels good

because the sun is staying out

but new storms could
    be coming later
on
we go down
    the street
    and bring grandma
    back to our house
to stay the night

to stay together

over in aunt nina's yard

there is a tree
    the roots
          are half the size
          of our living
               room
and higher than our roof

    just lying there
a hundred year old
               tree

it takes a long time
      to get to sleep

with many hugs
and drinks of
                    water
and bathroom trips

it takes a long time
because the radio
is bringing news

the streets are blocked
and only ambulances can
get in and out
there are people missing

there are red lights
flashing down the block
but daddy says
        the beds
are safe

it still takes a long time

in the morning

    the sky is blue
and it is   school
          again

hungry
hungry   hurry
        up

at our school

   the skylights have big holes
through their glass panes
      there is glass all over
all the floors

it is a day for wearing shoes
even on the mats

from the upstairs windows

we can see
     one injured family
walking in the street
   not feeling much
when these
rescue guys
     take them by
    the arms   to
the ambulance

they have to think
about their names

we can see a house

the top two floors
            had been blown
                    away
the back of the house
is gone
            and the front
is mostly
    gone

but in a corner of the front
                    room
the table is still set
                for dinner
and the silverware   is neatly
    on the napkins

    the glasses

are

        still

        standing

the firemen start yelling

get away from there
                    these
buildings
            can fall
at any time

will have to be
knocked
down   as soon as the people
        move their things away

        one girl   is carrying
                her   winter coat
                her   boots
        out to a truck

        one boy   is playing
                where
                his
                house   had been
                        is not

you can see

a broken house
a street of broken
        houses
a broken baby doll
  in the boards

dogs and cats
    are
        sniffing
        hungry
    and
cows are strolling
down the
      street

the woman

is telling about the wind

it was not just   the wind
and the pressure
                    on your back
                    on your head
you couldn't get up
you couldn't
                    move

but the wind was full of dirt
and sand   and filth and rocks
              so many bits of
                            glass
and heavy things

        heavy things
              in the
                    air

momma says

that's why
the funnel
    cloud
   is
      black

         not the
         color
            of
       the
          wind

but dirt and boards
and trees
    and stones

it moved

        down the main street
        and along the railroad
               tracks
all across the
         flat
new section
of the town

new streets of houses
old streets

up the highway
to the college

to the end

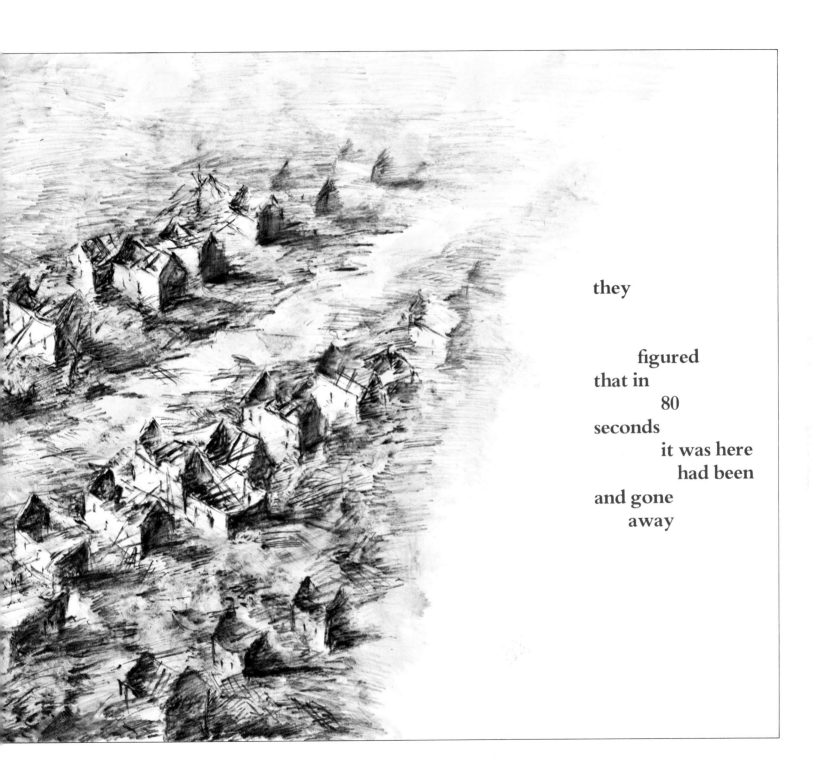

they

        figured
that in
      80
seconds
       it was here
        had been
and gone
   away

daddy says

he spent the day
                    out on the streets
then came back home   for dinner

one part of town
                    the chain saws
work all day cutting up the trees
                    that block the streets

a mile away   the people
   mowing lawns
on a green   spring
                    evening

late past bedtime

we are meeting
                    around
the kitchen
        table

the wind is blowing from the west again
    and the creaking branches of the
                                    big
            tree in the yard
                        make
                            their
                        moans

the windows rattle
    like another storm
is coming
            and everything outside
                is much too   loud
                    for
                        bedtime

daddy says

there will be
storms for many springs
for many summers

momma says
we can be tougher
than some thunder
noise
some   flash

grandma
says
the last time one came
through here was fifty
years ago   and   i   can
wait another   fifty
for the next

brother says

        it never seems to rain
        in a quiet way out here
just water
      for the garden
and the corn fields
when they get   dry

just wet
  no
     wind
        it never seems to rain
        in a quiet
            way

i say
     that's right
     good
        night

and anyway

        no
         old
       tornado
i don't care
     how
     bad

       is stronger
than the
    people on the land

Epilogue

These *Tornado Poems* were begun after the Xenia tornado of April 3, 1974. A few miles away, in Yellow Springs, we lived through the wind and hailstones that the storm produced. The funnels passed us by. We were safe. But we spent that evening, and most of the night, waiting for new outbreaks of storms and listening to reports of destruction and tragedy. After the roads were opened, we were able to see results of the force of the tornado and talk with witnesses and rescue workers.

The Xenia tornado was part of a massive outbreak of tornadoes that struck thirteen states during a sixteen-hour period. From 1 P.M. on April 3 through 5 A.M. the following morning, 148 tornadoes were recorded. Their paths covered more than 2,500 miles. Three hundred people were killed and another 5,400 injured. Over 50,000 people were affected as the tornadoes traveled from Alabama, Tennessee, Kentucky, Illinois, and Indiana, through Georgia, North Carolina, Ohio, Michigan and into Canada. Other states hit were Mississippi, West Virginia, Virginia, and New York – states not usually affected by tornadoes.

This outbreak of storms has been called by scientists a "once-in-a-century" event. In Tennessee, a tornado dropped into a 1,000-foot river canyon and swept back up on the other side. In Kentucky, one left a path five miles wide. A tornado traveled 3,300 feet high, over Betty Mountain in the Blue Ridge Mountains between Georgia and North Carolina. In Indiana, one tornado continued on its path for 121 miles before it lifted back up to the sky. Six towns were struck twice, and damage everywhere was in the many millions of dollars. But the Xenia tornado was one of the strongest and most damaging of this unprecedented "super-outbreak." Thirty-three people were killed and whole sections of the town were destroyed.

Each spring and summer there are many tornadoes in the South, Midwest, and some eastern states. In late February and early March, when winter breaks and there are occasional warm spells, we begin to listen more carefully to the weather reports each day, and to watch the sky.

These poems are about one tornado during one series of tragic storms. But they are meant for all who have experienced or read about any tornado – any natural disaster. These poems are dedicated to the people of Xenia, Ohio, who are rebuilding, and to people everywhere who survive and overcome forces greater than them-selves. We really are stronger.

ARNOLD ADOFF
September 10, 1976

About the Author

ARNOLD ADOFF is an anthologist and poet who is well-known for the uniqueness of his work and who seeks to find a new visual and verbal means of expression. Here he has presented through poetry a poignant statement of survival in the face of one of nature's most devastating forces. Mr. Adoff lives in Yellow Springs, Ohio, with his wife, novelist Virginia Hamilton, and their two children. Among his anthologies are *Brothers and Sisters* and *Black Out Loud*, which are available in Dell Laurel-Leaf paperback editions. *Tornado!* is his second book in collaboration with Ronald Himler. The first, *make a circle keep us in,* was a Kirkus Choice for 1975.

About the Artist

RONALD HIMLER has illustrated many books for children, among them *Morris Brookside, a Dog,* available in a Yearling edition. With each new book, Mr. Himler tries to use a technique that will best define the text. Here he has broadened and deepened his techniques to express a mood of hope and determination. Mr. Himler lives in New York City with his wife, Ann, and their children.

About the Book

This book has been designed by Lynn Braswell. The text was set in Bembo by Arrow Typographers, Inc. The book was printed by Holyoke Lithograph Co., Inc., and bound by Economy Bookbinding Corporation.